Historic
SCOTLAND
❧ PEOPLE ❧
AND PLACES

Historic SCOTLAND

PEOPLE AND PLACES

David J. Breeze

B. T. BATSTFORD LTD/HISTORIC SCOTLAND

First Published 2002

©Text David Breeze 2002

Photography by David Henrie and Mike Brooks

ISBN 07134 8615 5

A CIP catalogue record for this book is available from the British Library.

Printed in Italy by G. Canale & C. S.p.A.

for the publishers

B T Batsford

64 Brewery Road

London N7 9NY

England

www.batsford.com

A member of **Chrysalis** Books plc

CONTENTS

and other islands that we believe were the Shetland Islands. Indeed, Pytheas of Marseilles 300 years earlier had sailed to the north of Scotland, the point he called the Orcas promontory. There he learnt that six days' sailing to the north lay a place called Thule, possibly Shetland but perhaps either western Norway or Iceland. This points to considerable local geographical knowledge.

Coin bearing the head of Claudius.

A N T O N I N E
W A L L

A Roman cavalryman

In July 138 the Emperor Hadrian died and his chosen successor, Antoninus Pius, ascended to the purple. Antoninus Pius had never held an army command but was now emperor of the greatest state in the western world and commander-in-chief of an army approaching half-a-million strong. It may be that he decided to conduct a limited war of aggression in Britain in order to strengthen his position on the throne. Certainly, preparations were already in progress at Corbridge by Hadrian's Wall in 139.

Victory over the tribes of southern Scotland was celebrated in the conventional manner by religious ceremonies, distribution of medals and erection of monuments. The Antonine Wall was constructed in the aftermath of the victory. Forty Roman miles long, it stretched from Bo'ness on the Forth to Old Kilpatrick on the Clyde and consisted of a turf rampart fronted by a wide and deep ditch with forts

roughly every 2 miles (3 km) apart. It was built in the 140s and abandoned about 20 years later when the army returned to Hadrian's Wall. One of the forts on the Wall lay at Rough Castle (see above) overlooking the Rowan Tree Burn. The ditch of the Antonine Wall lies in shadow to the left of centre with the west rampart and ditches of the fort running away to the right.

A monument was placed at modern Bo'ness towards the eastern end of the newly constructed Antonine Wall. It displays (see right) a Roman cavalryman riding down four naked enemies, one already decapitated.

A traditional triumphal scene on the Bridgeness Distance Slab.

WHITHORN PRIORY

St Ninian

It was sometime around 400 – perhaps a few years later – that Ninian came to Whithorn to establish his mission. He built a church of stone, called Candida Casa, the white house, dedicated to St Martin of Tours who had died in 397. Ninian may not have been the first Christian in Scotland, but he is the first known missionary.

Whithorn is the oldest ecclesiastical place in Scotland, and one of the most famous. Its reputation drew many pilgrims, including Robert the Bruce and several of the Stewart kings. Mary Queen of Scots stayed here on the night of 10 August 1563 on her return from her progress through south-west Scotland.

Whithorn became the seat of the Bishop of Galloway. At the Reformation the bishop turned Protestant, and the priory was abandoned, but the nave of the church, the entrance to which is shown here, survived and remained in use until a new church was built in 1822. Beside it are the remains of the medieval crypt, similar to those that still survive at Glasgow, Hexham and Ripon, and which formerly held the relics of saints.

Above: Douglas Strachan designed this stained-glass window of St Ninian for St Margaret's Chapel, Edinburgh Castle in 1922. Left: The twelfth-century doorway at Whithorn.

Douglas Strachan's
stained-glass
window of
St Columba in
St Margaret's
Chapel,
Edinburgh Castle.

IONA ABBEY

St Columba (d 597)

St Columba was an Irishman, but in 563, for reasons that are not totally clear, he left his native land and went to Argyll with 12 companions. Soon after his arrival he established a monastery on Iona. We know little about Columba's monastery. Nearly a century after his death, one of Columba's successors, Adomnán, wrote a life of

16

the saint and described the site, recording that it included a church, a communal building for the monks, a guest house and sleeping-places. Columba, it was said, slept on the bare rock with a stone for his pillow.

Columba died on Iona in 597 but over the following two centuries his foundation flourished. Its sanctity became so revered that it was used as the burial place for Scottish kings until the late eleventh century when the Hebrides were formally ceded to the kings of Norway. However, in 795 the Vikings attacked Iona and on several occasions over the following decades it was plundered, its buildings burnt and its monks murdered.

Around the year 1200, Reginald, son of Somerled, re-established the monastery under the Benedictine monks. They erected a completely new church and monastic buildings which survived, with repair and modification, until the Reformation in 1560. Thereafter these great buildings became a romantic ruin until, in 1899, the Duke of Argyll passed ownership to the Iona Cathedral Trust on condition that the church be restored for worship. Today, Iona Abbey is a spiritual home to many modern pilgrims.

MEIGLE SYMBOL STONE

A Pict

Those forebears whose names and deeds are known to us, some of whom appear in this book, form a very small part of our ancestry. Most of our predecessors are anonymous and it is appropriate that we do not know the name of this Pictish horseman, just one representative of the various nations which came together to form the kingdom of the Scots in the Middle Ages.

The Picts were the descendants of the prehistoric peoples of Scotland and occupied that part of the country called Caledonia by the Roman writer Tacitus in the first century AD. Two hundred years later, in 297, we first hear of the Picts, the painted people. Their kingdom grew to cover all land north of the Forth-Clyde isthmus and their sculpture has been found in Orkney, Shetland and the Western Isles as well as mainland Scotland. It forms one of the most distinctive and most important parts of our inheritance from the early historic period.

The horse steps out in style with the rider sitting on a striped saddle-cloth and holding reins. His cloak partly obscures his sword, which has a rounded chape, while his shoes are visible below. In his right hand he holds a spear. This horseman is one of many such depictions of Picts that date, perhaps, from the eighth century. The front of this stone is adorned by a cross, a clear indication that by this time the Picts had been converted to Christianity.

SUENO'S STONE

Dubh (king 962–7)

On the edge of Forres stands a great stone monolith, now protected within a glass shelter. It was found buried here in 1726 and re-erected. It was then named after the Danish king Sweyn Forkbeard.

On one side is a cross, covered, as is the rest of this face, with interlace. The other side bears a great scene, or rather four scenes, depicting a battle. Both cavalry and infantry, as well as archers, took part in the battle. In one panel (near left) a curved object is shown, below which lie decapitated bodies and severed heads.

The style of Sueno's Stone suggests that it dates from the ninth or tenth century. At that time Scotland was under pressure from the Vikings, but there were also internal fights, in particular between the kings of the Scots and the mormaers or earls of Moray. In one battle, in 966, Dubh, King of the Scots, was killed at Forres and his body laid beneath the bridge before burial. It is possible that the curved object is the bridge and the head in the box that of King Dubh.

Sueno's Stone has suffered severely from weathering during the 250 years since its re-erection. As it was considered too delicate to move, the Stone was protected by a shelter in 1991.

THE PEEL RING OF LUMPHANAN

Macbeth (king 1040–57)

It is hard today to see past Shakespeare's depiction of Macbeth to the real man. We know little of Macbeth, but it is clear that his reign was more peaceful than Shakespeare would have us believe.

For 200 years, since the creation of the united Kingdom of the Picts and the Scots in about 843, the Scottish kingship had passed between alternate branches of the royal family. Malcolm II, who had no sons, subverted this by ensuring the succession of his grandson Duncan. Macbeth, we believe, was a member of another branch of the royal family. In 1040 he overthrew Duncan, and went on to reign for 17 years. During this time, in 1050, he felt secure enough in his kingdom to visit Rome, a journey of many months.

Duncan's eldest son, Malcolm Canmore (Great Chief), managed to overthrow Macbeth, who fled to his family heartland in Moray. He was killed in battle at Lumphanan on 15 August 1057. Malcolm III Canmore and his descendants managed to overthrow the previous arrangements for succession and establish the right of primogeniture.

The castle known as the Peel Ring was built close to the place where Macbeth died, but 250 years later. The site of the castle is shown here.

Actor Derek Jacobi as Macbeth in the stage production at Stratford-upon-Avon.

ST MAGNUS' CHURCH, EGILSAY

St Magnus (d 1117)

In about 780 the first Norse raiders, the Vikings, arrived in Orkney and soon established an earldom that was to survive until 1468 when it was 'returned' to Scotland, a country which had not existed in 780.

The earldom was often split between different branches of the family and sometimes the earls quarrelled. In 1117 the earls – cousins – Hakon and Magnus agreed to meet on the island of Egilsay to settle their differences. Magnus, however, found that he had been tricked by Hakon who arrived with eight ships. Magnus spent the night in prayer and on the following day surrendered to his cousin who had him executed.

The church on Egilsay is believed to have been erected to the memory of Magnus. Its round tower is unusual for Scotland, but such towers are found elsewhere in the countries that fringe the North Sea.

In time, Magnus received an even greater memorial: the cathedral erected in his honour by his nephew and heir, Earl, later St, Rognvald. In 1137 the body of Magnus was transported from Birsay, where it had originally been buried, to Kirkwall and the building of the cathedral commenced. On 13 December 1142 Magnus' bones were reburied in the cathedral. In 1919 a box of Norwegian pine was found in a pier on the south side of the choir, the skull inside still bearing the marks of the axe which killed the saint.

Stained-glass window of St Magnus in Lerwick Town Hall, dating to the 1880s

24

KELSO ABBEY

David I (king 1124–53)

King David I founded or re-established more than ten monasteries and priories in Scotland. One of these lay at Selkirk where he brought monks of the Tironensian Order in about 1113. The Tironensians were a new order created at Tiron near Chartres by St Bernard of Tiron. David, impressed by what he had heard, set out to visit St Bernard, who died before he arrived. David, however, did return with a group of monks. These were the first monks of any reformed order to settle anywhere in the British Isles. The monastery was moved to Kelso in 1128, probably so that it was closer to the important royal castle of Roxburgh.

At Kelso David erected an abbey that grew into one of the wealthiest in Scotland, no doubt aided by its proximity to Roxburgh Castle. The abbey also had a church of unusual plan with a western as well as an eastern transept. Only the western transept survives today, with part of the tower over the crossing. A description of the abbey in 1517 still survives in the Vatican archives.

David I shown in old age on a charter of 1159 granted to Kelso Abbey.

David also started the process of dividing Scotland into parishes, creating the framework that survives to this day. He established many burghs that were the bases for his new legal and administrative organisation for the country.

BISHOP'S PALACE KIRKWALL

Hakon IV of Norway (king 1217–63)

For over 650 years parts of Scotland owed allegiance to a foreign crown. About 780 the Vikings from Norway arrived in Orkney. The earldom they established in Orkney and Shetland was not incorporated into the Scottish kingdom until 1468/9. The Norwegian crown had to struggle to maintain its control over these and other far-flung territories that extended over the north Atlantic – and against a Scotland growing in strength.

King Hakon IV depicted on a seal.

It was in the face of the expansionism of King Alexander III of Scotland (reigned 1249–86) that King Hakon IV Hakonson, the last of the great Norwegian sea-kings, depicted on this seal, assembled a great fleet and sailed westward to seek to maintain his authority. His venture fizzled out at the 'battle' of Largs (little more than a skirmish in reality) in 1263. Hakon retired to Orkney where he died at midnight on the night of 15/16 December in his bishop's palace in Kirkwall, shown right. His body was laid to rest in the cathedral beyond and in the following Spring it was taken to Bergen where it was buried in Christ Church beside his own royal palace: his great hall within that palace, Hakonshalle, still survives. His great granddaughter, Margaret, Maid of Norway, also died in Orkney and was buried in the same church in Bergen 26 years later.

INCHMAHOME PRIORY

Walter Stewart (d *c* 1295)

In this delightful double effigy dating from about 1295, Walter Stewart, Earl of Menteith, faces his countess. They were buried at Inchmahome in the priory founded in 1238 by Walter Comyn, an earlier Earl of Menteith, for the Augustinian canons, known as the Black Canons from the colour of their habit. The main picture shows the cloisters with the chapter-house beyond.

Inchmahome later came into the hands of the Erskine family. The Erskines had the responsibility for bringing up the royal children, and the infant Mary Queen of Scots was placed in the care of John, Lord Erskine at Stirling Castle in 1543. In 1547, when the army of King Henry VIII of England ravaged southern Scotland, Lord Erskine moved the queen for safety to Inchmahome Priory, where his son was the commendator (lay administrator). Inchmahome was a sanctuary for the queen in three senses: it was an island, a religious house, and through the Erskine connection a family house. Robert, the commendator, paid for his family's support for the queen through his death at the Battle of Pinkie fighting the English invasion. His brother, John, who succeeded at Inchmahome, became guardian to Mary's son, James VI, and, indeed, was the only one of the four regents for James VI who was to die in his bed.

SWEETHEART
ABBEY

Devorguilla (d 1290)

Devorguilla so loved her husband, John Balliol, that on his death she had his heart embalmed and placed in an ivory casket to be kept with her. On her death it was buried with her. On her effigy in Sweetheart Abbey, she is depicted holding it in her hands.

Sweetheart was founded by Devorguilla in 1273, the last Cistercian house to be created in Scotland. She also endowed Balliol College, Oxford, established by her husband. Devorguilla was descended from King David I and it was through her that her ill-fated son, King John (1292–6) inherited his claim to the throne.

Her husband, John Balliol, was a great
landowner with estates in France and England as
well as Scotland: Barnard Castle in County Durham
was an important Balliol stronghold. It was on his
French estates that King John died after his
expulsion from Scotland. Devorguilla spent much
of her long widowhood on her own Huntingdon
estates, at Fotheringhay, where Mary Queen of Scots
was to be executed in 1587.

CAMBUSKENNETH ABBEY

Robert the Bruce (king 1306–29)

The fine bell tower is almost all that survives above ground of Cambuskenneth Abbey. A unique survival in Scotland, it was probably built shortly before 1300.

The abbey was founded in 1147, probably by King David I: its name may commemorate an event associated with an earlier Scottish king, perhaps Kenneth McAlpin, the founder of the royal house.

The proximity of the abbey to the royal castle of Stirling (in the background) ensured that Cambuskenneth's abbots played a full part in the affairs of the kingdom and the abbey itself was often the scene of important events. In 1308 several Scottish barons met to swear allegiance to Robert the Bruce, crowned at Scone two years before. King Robert himself was present in 1326 when a Parliament was held at Cambuskenneth, the first to be attended by burgesses. On this occasion all swore fealty to Robert's son, David, and to his grandson, David's successor, Robert Stewart, who was to be the first king of a new dynasty. These affairs of state were completed by the marriage of the king's sister, Christian, to Sir Andrew Moray of Bothwell.

Seal of Robert I.

DUNDONALD CASTLE

Robert II (king 1371–99)

The Stewart family originated in Brittany where they were hereditary stewards of the lords of Dol. After service in England, Walter joined the household of David I and in 1160 was appointed High Steward to William I. His lands lay on the southern shore of the Clyde and were a bulwark against the Norse who then occupied the Hebrides. At Paisley, Walter founded an abbey where many of his descendants are buried.

James the Steward supported Bruce, and his son, Walter, married the king's daughter Marjory. For much of his life their son, Robert, was heir to either his grandfather or his younger uncle. He eventually succeeded to the crown at the age of 54, but was not one of Scotland's more successful kings.

It was probably the first Walter who built the original castle at Dundonald. Its successor was replaced by the present castle, which was erected by King Robert II, perhaps to mark his accession to the throne. The castle commands a wide view towards the west, and it was on the western face that the arms of the king and his wife were placed. The blue and white checked band on the Stewart coat of arms is a reminder of the origin of the family, being a representation of the checked cloth used for counting money.

A coin of Robert II.

37

INCHCOLM
ABBEY

Walter Bower (d 1449)

King Alexander I (1107–24) is said to have intended to found an abbey on the island of Inchcolm in thanks for the safety offered by the island's hermit in a storm. However, the abbey was yet another foundation of his younger brother David. The abbey had a turbulent history owing to its exposed position in the Firth of Forth, the storms coming not just from the sea but also from English invaders.

It was during one such unsettled period that one of Inchcolm's greatest sons compiled a book, which is a prime source for Scottish medieval history. The book is the *Scotichronicon* and the author was Abbot Walter Bower. Bower had been created abbot in 1418, but he did not start to write until 1441. His history incorporates the earlier history written by John Fordun and takes up the story from the reign of Malcolm III Canmore (1057–93), ending with the death of James I in 1437. The *Scotichronicon* is not just an important book on Scottish history as Bower described contemporary events, not least the English raids. It was perhaps his personal experience that led Bower to favour a renewal of the Auld Alliance with France. He died in 1449 and was buried in his beloved abbey.

The *Scotichronicon* contains some delightful illustrations. The image on the left shows the ship carrying Scota from Egypt. Scota was believed to be a daughter of a pharaoh who fled Egypt at the time of Moses carrying the Stone of Destiny with her: her descendants later came to Scotland via Spain and Ireland, naming their new home after their ancestress.

LINLITHGOW PALACE

Margaret Tudor (1489–1541)

A royal manor house may have existed at Linlithgow from the time of King David I, but a fire in 1424 destroyed whatever sat on the site. James I started to build a new palace and his work was continued by several of his successors down to James VI.

James IV erected the west range and remodelled the south range, building a new transe or corridor in an English style. In 1503 James married Margaret Tudor, daughter of Henry VII of England, and it is possible that English masons worked on the palace. The palace was given to the new queen and it was here in 1513 she learnt of the death of her husband at the Battle of Flodden where he had fallen fighting the army of her brother, Henry VIII. This marriage, however, ultimately brought the great-grandson of James IV and Margaret Tudor, James VI of Scotland and I of England, to the thrones of England and Ireland in 1603.

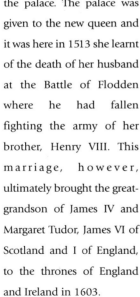

Linlithgow Palace and, left, the Church of St Michael. The painting of Margaret Tudor is by Daniel Mytens.

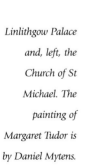

40

ST ANDREWS CASTLE

Cardinal David Beaton (1494–1546)

Cardinal David Beaton was a member of a powerful church family. Nephew of James Beaton, Archbishop of Glasgow and later St Andrews, he himself was Archbishop of St Andrews and uncle of another James Beaton, the last Roman Catholic Archbishop of Glasgow. These were not only leaders of the church, they also held high state offices. The first James was Treasurer and Chancellor of Scotland, while David aspired to be Regent of Scotland on the death of the king.

The family also personified the Franco-Scottish alliance, supported by James during the reign of James V, when David was educated in Paris, receiving a French bishopric. Nephew James fled to France at the Reformation in 1560 to spend the remaining 43 years of his life in Paris. Here he re-founded the Scots' College to educate Scots Roman Catholics.

David Beaton reached the highest level in the Church, being made a cardinal in 1538, then going on to become Archbishop of St Andrews soon afterwards. In 1546 he arrested the Protestant preacher George Wishart, had him tried for heresy and burnt at the stake. In revenge, the Fife lairds captured Beaton in his castle at St Andrews and hung him from his own castle window. The castle was later besieged by the Regent Arran and, on capture, several of the inmates, including John Knox, were sentenced to labour in a French galley.

ST CLEMENT'S CHURCH, RODEL

Alasdair Crotach (d 1547)

The church at Rodel on the southern point of the island of Harris was built in the early sixteenth century by the MacLeods of Dunvegan and Harris. Constructed of local stone, it is cruciform in plan with a large western tower. The church is placed over a local geological fault, which still causes tensions in the fabric of the building.

Alasdair MacLeod, 8th Lord of Harris and Dunvegan, erected his own tomb in the church in 1528, breaking with his family's tradition of burial on Iona. He was nicknamed Crotach, hump-backed, as a result of an injury sustained in battle with the MacDonalds of Clanranald. Alasdair was buried in Rodel in 1547.

The tomb is one of the finest in the Highlands. The effigy of Alasdair Crotach is in armour, with the feet resting on a crocodile. The arch is decorated with angels, saints and symbols of the apostles. Within the recess are depictions of a castle, possibly Alasdair Crotach's own castle at Dunvegan in Skye, a bishop, the Virgin and Child, St Clement, and a galley, part of the MacLeod arms. The galley is a reminder that the sea was – and is – the main means of communication between these western islands and it features in the coats of arms of the main families of the western seaboard.

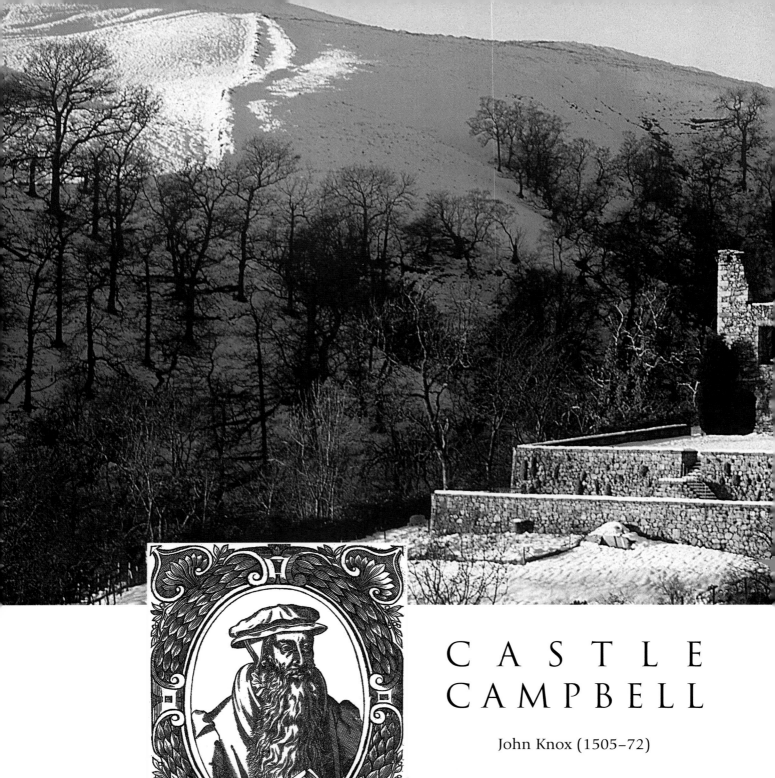

C A S T L E
C A M P B E L L

John Knox (1505–72)

John Knox, a native of Haddington and one of the
leaders of the Protestant Reformation, was educated
at St Andrews University before being ordained in
1536. After his labour in a French galley (see page

42), Knox went to live in England, where he became a parish priest, and subsequently Frankfurt and Geneva. He returned to Scotland in 1559, where he became Edinburgh's first Protestant minister. He died in Edinburgh in 1572.

In 1566 Knox came to Castle Campbell as the guest of the Earl of Argyll. He stayed several days and preached at the castle. Knox's host was Archibald Campbell, 5th Earl of Argyll, brother-in-law of Mary Queen of Scots. The castle and estates had been acquired about 100 years before by Colin Campbell,

1st Earl of Argyll, and it was probably then that the first surviving stone buildings were erected at the site formerly known as Castle Gloom.

The Campbells were strong supporters of the Reformation and, later, the Covenant. The 1st Marquis suffered the indignity of having his castle attacked by Montrose in 1645. Even worse, in 1654 the castle was sacked and burnt by General Monk, acting on behalf of Oliver Cromwell.

Knox is best known through this engraving published in Theodore Beza's *Icones* in 1580.

BLACKNESS CASTLE

James Hamilton,
2nd Earl of Arran (*c* 1516–75)

Blackness was a royal castle, helping to protect the Firth of Forth, a great sea inlet that offered potential invaders a route into central Scotland. Like many such fortresses, it also served as a state prison on occasions. Cardinal Beaton (*qv*) was briefly here in 1543, as was the Earl of Angus in the following year.

James Hamilton, 2nd Earl of Arran, was, for much of his life, heir to King James V, Queen Mary or her son James VI. His position led him to the regency of Scotland during the minority of Mary, 1543–54. As regent he had the right to use the royal palaces and castles and he brought his family to Blackness Castle, which he occupied as one of his main residences from 1543 to 1548. In 1548 the castle was occupied by the French and it remained in their hands until 1560 when, by the Treaty of Edinburgh, most French and English forces withdrew from Scotland.

Hamilton and his family generally supported Mary during the troubles of her reign and after. However, he disliked her marriage to Darnley for the queen's new

husband supplanted Hamilton as the first prince in the kingdom, and, together with the queen's half-brother James Stewart, Earl of Moray, he came out in rebellion. Moray supplied the brains and Hamilton the brawn, but their show of strength was easily defeated by the queen and the new king and the conspirators fled to England. They soon returned to Scotland, but Hamilton never regained his former power.

In 1549 Hamilton was created Duke of Châtelherault by King Henry II of France: he thus became the only duke in Scotland at that time and was often referred to simply as 'the Duke'. Although the estates were subsequently lost, the title was retained by the family and is now held by the Duke of Abercorn as heir male of the Hamiltons. Quite bizarrely, in 1864, the Emperor Napoleon III of France acknowledged his cousin, the Duke of Hamilton, who was actually a Douglas, as Duke of Châtelherault, effectively creating a second title.

CRICHTON CASTLE

James Hepburn,
4th Earl of Bothwell
(*c* 1535–78)

Crichton Castle was founded by the family of that name about 1400. One member became Chancellor of Scotland in the minority of King James II and it was to him that we owe the appearance of much of the castle today.

Crichton came into the hands of the Hepburn family in 1488. In 1556 James Hepburn succeeded to the castle and to the title, Earl of Bothwell. Four years later, in January 1562, he was host at the wedding of his sister Janet to John Stewart, half-brother of Mary Queen of Scots, at Crichton. There was 'much good sport and many pastimes', witnessed by the queen herself.

In 1567 Bothwell and Mary were themselves married at the Palace of Holyroodhouse only three months after the murder of the queen's second husband, Darnley: this painting was executed in the previous year. Bothwell's triumph was short-lived for a month later, in the face of the opposition of his fellow lords, Mary surrendered at Carberry and was

imprisoned in Lochleven Castle, while her new husband fled into exile: he was imprisoned in Draxholm Castle in Denmark where he died in 1578.

Some years later, Francis, son of Lord John and Lady Janet Stewart and nephew of both Mary and Bothwell, was able to enter into his inheritance, becoming 5th Earl of Bothwell. He remodelled Crichton Castle in an Italianate style, but offended his sovereign and fled abroad in 1595. His son sold the castle.

ABERDOUR
CASTLE

James Douglas,
4th Earl of Morton (d 1581)

Aberdour is one of the oldest surviving castles in Scotland, the earliest masonry dating to the Mortimer ownership before 1200. In 1342 it came into the hands of the Douglas family, who still own it.

Aberdour's most famous occupant was James Douglas, 4th Earl of Morton. Married to a cousin of Mary Queen of Scots, he was her chancellor; yet he was a conspirator in the murder of David Riccio at her Palace of Holyroodhouse in 1566. As a result he fled abroad. Morton was soon back in Scotland and played a prominent part in the events surrounding the queen's forced abdication in 1567. He was subsequently regent for her son, James VI, and it is from this time that his portrait dates. In 1581 he was executed on a trumped-up charge.

It was probably Morton who laid out the terraced garden and built the central range of the castle. Originally harled (a lime covering), it had three storeys, with private apartments for the earl and countess on the upper floor above a kitchen and storeroom.

A few years after his death, the lands and title of the Earl of Morton came to a cousin, Sir William Douglas of Lochleven, the custodian of Queen Mary during her imprisonment at Lochleven Castle from June 1567 to May 1568. It was his grandson who erected the east range which contained his picture gallery on the first floor.

LOCHLEVEN CASTLE

George, 5th Lord Seton (*c* 1530–85)

George Seton was one of Mary Queen of Scots' closest advisors. He attended her wedding to the Dauphin Francis in 1558 and on her return to Scotland in 1561 became Master of the Household: he is depicted here in his robes of office. He helped her escape from Holyroodhouse after the murder of Riccio, was with her at Carberry, and helped organise her escape from her island prison of Lochleven Castle on 2 May 1568. Seton met the queen when she landed and, attended by a large body of horse, took her to his castle at Niddrie to the west of Edinburgh. Here she issued a proclamation to rally her supporters before moving on to Hamilton where she took refuge on the lands of her cousin, the Earl of Arran. Seton was with her army and was taken prisoner when it was defeated at the Battle of Langside. Indeed, Seton held to the queen's cause until its collapse with the capture of Mary's last stronghold, Edinburgh Castle, in 1572.

The queen was well acquainted with Lochleven Castle before her imprisonment there, having been the guest of Sir William Douglas on several occasions. It was while at Lochleven Castle that Mary was forced to abdicate on 24 July 1567 shortly after she miscarried twins by the Earl of Bothwell, her third husband.

DUNDRENNAN ABBEY

Mary Queen of Scots
(queen 1542–67, executed 1587)

Mary Queen of Scots bust by the French artist Ponce Jacquio.

No book on Scottish history would be complete without reference to Mary Queen of Scots, yet she left little permanent impact on the buildings of her country. Dundrennan Abbey, therefore, the place where Mary spent her last night on Scottish soil, 15 May 1568, is an appropriate building to commemorate Scotland's tragic queen. Mary fled here from defeat at Langside a few days before, having spent the previous 11 months imprisoned in Lochleven Castle on an island in the middle of the loch of that name. After Dundrennan Mary knew nothing but the inside of other prisons.

Mary crossed the Solway to England of her own volition and with insufficient concern for the consequences. Ten years before, she had refused to acknowledge the accession of Elizabeth and the English queen had little choice but to keep her rival under close supervision.

Mary was to spend the next 19 years in custody. Her last prison, and the place of her execution on 9 February 1587, was Fotheringhay Castle. It is one of the quirks of history that this lay on the lands of the Earldom of Huntingdon held by her ancestor King David I, while it was at Fotheringhay in 1163 that another ancestor, Walter Fitzalan, Steward to William I, signed the charter establishing the abbey at Paisley.

This bust was executed in happier days, towards the end of Mary's stay in France when she was queen of both France and Scotland. This is indicated by the closed imperial crown she wears.

from 1547 to 1596. In 1584 William Forbes responded to the spirit of the times by building himself a new house beside his ancient fortified tower, which lies to the left above. The work took five and a half years to complete and was built under the direction of the master-mason Thomas Leiper, whose initials survive on a skewput. His new residence had a fortified air, but this was largely for show.

The new buildings were arranged round a courtyard. The three ranges contained the main hall, the laird's private quarters, a gallery containing his library, bedrooms, kitchen, bakehouse and brewhouse – outside lay the dovecot. As befitting his local status, the castle contained a prison. William Forbes laid out a formal garden beyond his walls, to the west and south of his home.

William Forbes not only provided for himself and his wife in life, but also in death, building a tomb for them both in the local churchyard. He remains commemorated in stone at his own castle.

LAUDERDALE AISLE

John, Lord Maitland
(d 1595)
John, 1st Earl of Lauderdale
(d 1645)

The Maitlands of Lethington were great servants of the Crown in the sixteenth and seventeenth centuries. William (d 1573) served as Secretary of State to Mary Queen of Scots and travelled the length and breadth of the country with his mistress. His younger brother, John (d 1595), was also a supporter of the queen. Both brothers were with the queen's party in Edinburgh Castle when it was besieged after Mary's flight to England. William died in a prison in Leith shortly after the castle's surrender in 1573; John was similarly imprisoned for his support for the queen, in his case in Tantallon Castle.

John was reconciled with James VI and served as Lord Privy Seal, Secretary of State and Lord Chancellor. He accompanied his king to Norway and Denmark to bring back James' bride, Anne of Denmark, and was created Lord Maitland. His son, John, was raised to the peerage as Earl of Lauderdale, and his grandson, also John, was made Duke of Lauderdale for his support for Charles I and Charles II during the Civil War.

Lethington survives to this day, renamed Lennoxlove on the instructions of Frances Duchess of Richmond and Lennox in memory of her husband. It is now the home of the Duke of Hamilton, a member of another great family which has provided many royal servants over the centuries.

John, 1st Lord Maitland, and his son, John, 1st Earl of Lauderdale, were buried with their wives in the Lauderdale Aisle in the church of St Mary, Haddington.

CONSILIO ET ANIMIS
ANIMIS
CONSILIO ET ANIMIS

ANNÆ MÆTELANÆ, IOANNIS BARONIS DE THYRLESTANE, SCO. CAN. ET IANÆ
FLAMINIÆ, FILIÆ, PVELLÆ, NOBILIS, QVÆ, PIETATE, INGENIO, CASTITATE, ET
MORVM ELEGANTIA INSIGNIS, ROBERTO WINTONIÆ COMITI DESPONSATA,
VIRGO MORTVA EST. AN. 1609. PRID. NON. QVINTIL. ÆTACTO ÆTAT. AN. 19
EODEM CVM MATRE FVNERE ELATA.
IOANNES MÆTEILANVS, L. C. VNICÆ SORORI FRATER VNICVS M.P.

IANÆ. MÆTEILANÆ. VIRGINI LECTISSIMÆ, CVIVS DIVINO INGENIO, ATQ; INDVSTRIÆ, NIHIL DIFFICILE
VNQVAM EST VISVM, QVOD NOBILEM, PVDICAMQ; PVELLAM DECERET, CVIVS VERA PIETAS, ITA BENE
VENVSTAM, INDITA CASTITAS, MORVM SVAVITAS, ET INDOLIS PRÆCLARÆ ÆTATEM PRÆTER ÆTATEM
MIRABANTVRCVM INVENI VIX PARCABVM EXCIPIVNT.
IOANNES MÆTEILANVS, LAVDERIÆ COMES ET ISABELLA SETONIA PARENTES PRÆPOSTERO NATVRÆ
ORDINE SVPERSTITES D. DILECTI, INSEPERVM HOC MEMORIÆ SACR. STATVERVNT. VIXIT ANNOS 19
M. D. 8. VITAM MORTALEM EXVIT 6.10. DECEMB. 1651.

IANÆ. FLAMINIÆ. IACOBI BARONIS FLEMYNG.
EX BARBARA HAMILTONA, IACOBI DVCIS
CASTRI-ERALDI FILIA, PROLI VNICA. SERENISSIMÆ
HEROINÆ, CVIVS VIRILIS ANIMVS SECVNDIS IVXTA,
AC DVBIIS REBVS CONSTANS PERMANSIT; QVÆ
SVMMÆ ERGA DEVM REILIGIONIS, ERGA MARITV
FIDEI, AMORIS ERGA LIBEROS (DVOS ENIM
PEPERIT IOANNEM ET ANNAM MÆTEILAN)
NOBILITATIS DENIQ; ATQ; HVMANITATIS ERGA
OMNES, VIVENS, MORIENSQ; SINGVLARI PRÆLVXIT
EXEMPLO. QVÆ QVAMVIS SECVNDIS NVPTIIS
IOANNI CASSILISSÆ. COMITI IVNCTA HIC
TAMEN CVM PRIORE MARITO, EODEM SIMVL
CONDITORIO REPONI VOLVIT, INFELICI CALCVLO
EXTINCTA EDINBVRGI. 9. CAL. QVINTIL. 1609.
CVRRENTE ANNO ÆTATIS 55.

IOANNES MÆTEILANVS LAVDERIÆ COMES,
EIVS VNIGENA, PARENTIBVS OPT.
.... RE PIETATE QVA IMPENSA

ISABELLA SETONIA LAVDERIÆ COMITISSA,
ALEXANDRI FERMELINODVNI COMITIS, SCOTIÆ
CANCELLARII, ET D. LILIÆ DRVMMONDÆ FILIA, VIVA
GAVDIVM, MORTVA MARITI GEMITVS, HIC SITA EST;
QVÆ, MATRONARVM SPLENDOR, CONIVGVM HONOS,
PVDICITIÆ IVBAR, SANCTIMONIÆ TEMPLVM, VIRTVTVM
ET FORMÆ CVMVLVS, VIRVM (CVM QVO MIRABILI
CONCORDIA AN. 28. MENS. 4. TRANSEGIT) QVINDECIM
LIBERORVM NVMERO AVXIT, MARIVM 7. FÆMEIL. 8.
SVPERSTITIBVS TANTVM QVATVOR IOANNE, ROBERTO,
SOPHIA CAROLO; QVÆ SIC SEMPER VIXIT, VT SECVLVM
IPSA HAVD DIGNVM VIDERETVR, ITA DIEM EXTREMVM
CLAVSIT, VT MORS, OMNI VITÆ SVÆ CVRRICVLO
RESPONDERET; AC POST INCREDIBILEM IN LONGISS:
MORBO CONSTANTIAM, PATIENTIAM, PIETATEM, FESSI
CORPORIS ERGASTVLO SOLVTA, IN TERRIS, VT
CŒLO FRVERETVR, ESSE DESIIT. 2. NOVEMB. 1638.
ANNOS NATA 44 M.3.D.2.

IOANNES MÆTEILANVS LAVDERIÆ COMES,
CONIVX ....ISSIMÆ TANTÆ IACTVRÆ PROPEMODVM
INTOLE...... INCOMPARABILI, CVIVS MERITA
.... XVI

IOANNI MÆTEILANO BARONI DE THYRLESTANE MAGNO SCOTIÆ CANCELLARIO.
QVI A NOBILI MÆTEILANA STIRPE ORIVNDVS, VETVSTISSIMÆ FAMILIÆ DECVS
CELEBRIORE TITVLO AVXIT; CVIVS SINCERA PIETAS, HEROICA MENS, ERVDITIO
SINGVLARIS, GNAVA FORTITVDO, POSTERIS ÆMVLANDA, INVIDENDA ANTIQVIS, PAREM
VIX HABVERVNT; LIBERALITAS EXPROMPTA, LÆTVS LEPIDVSQ; INGENII VIGOR, DEVINXIT
SIBI PVBLICE OMNES PRIVATIM SINGVLOS. QVEM POST VARIA IN REP. PRÆCLARÈ GESTA
MVNIA, IACOBVS EIVS NOMINIS 6. SCOTORVM REX (OMNIVM QVOS ÆVROPA VSQVAM
VIDIT REGVM SAPIENTISSIMVS) AD SVMM CANCELLARIATVS FASTIGIVM, ACCLAMANTIBVS
TRIBVS REGNI ORDINIBVS, IN COMITIIS PVBLICIS EVEXIT: SED MVNVS ILLVD ANNOS VIX
NOVEM SVSTINVIT; CVM EA TAMEN PRVDENTIA, INTEGRITATE, AC LAVDE VT MERITO
AFFIRMARI POSSIT, BREVIS DIGNITATIS INGENTEM FVISSE GLORIAM. TANDEM ANNOS NATVS
QVINQVAGINTA, IN MEDIO FERE HONORVM ET VIRTVTVM CVRRICVLO EREPTVS, ACERBV
SVI DESIDERIVM RELIQVIT OMNIBVS; PRÆCIPVE REGI OPTIMO, QVI VERSIBVS
VERNACVLIS SVPREMO HVIC MARMORI INCISIS DEMORTVO PARENTAVIT.
OBIIT AN: 1595. 5. NON. OCTOB.
IN ARCE DE THYRLESTANE A SE RECENS EXSTRVCTA
IOANNES MÆTEILANVS LAVDERIÆ COMES, FILIVS VNIGENA, PARENTIBVS OPT.
MAIORE PIETATE QVAM IMPENSA P. C.

IOANNES MÆTEILANVS LAVDERIÆ COMES LOCVM DELEGIT SEPVL:
AD PARENTVM PEDES, SIBI ET VXORI ISABELLÆ SETONIÆ, NE QVOS
SINGVLARIS AMOR ET VNANIMIS VITÆ CONSVETVDO CONIVNXIT VEL
MORS IPSA SEIVNGERET TVMVLO.

HUNTLY
CASTLE

George Gordon,
6th Earl of Huntly (1562–1636)

Robert the Bruce granted Strathbogie to Sir Adam Gordon of Huntly in Berwickshire in 1314 in return for his loyalty. The Gordons became established in north-east Scotland, rising steadily through the peerage to a dukedom and in the process changing the name of the area from Strathbogie to the now familiar Huntly.

George became 6th Earl of Huntly in 1576. He rebelled against King James VI, but following his restoration to favour was created Marquis of Huntly in 1599. As befitting his new status, he improved his castle. Although he made improvements inside, it is the outside that claims our attention.

Along the top floor of the south range he added a series of oriel windows together with a belvedere in the adjacent round tower. Over the windows a frieze proudly spells out the name and rank of the owner and his wife:

GEORGE GORDON FIRST MARQVIS OF HUNTLIE 16

HENRIETTA STEWART MARQVESSE OF HUNTLIE 02

The marquis added one further touch. Over the entrance to his palace he placed an impressive frontispiece, wrought in stone, shown above right, a truly remarkable achievement for the stonemason.

Immediately above the doorway are the arms of the marquis and his wife, surmounted by those of the king and his wife. The square panel above held, until its destruction in 1640, the Five Wounds of Christ, and the round panel destroyed at the same time, the Risen Christ. At the summit, and now badly eroded, is St Michael. Thus the visitors to the castle raised their eyes to heaven and saw the importance of the lord of Huntly.

DUNFERMLINE PALACE

Charles 1 (b 1600; king 1625–49)

The abbey at Dunfermline was founded by Margaret, queen of Malcolm III. They, their family and successors down to Robert the Bruce in 1329 were buried in the abbey church erected by King David I.

One privilege of the descendants of the founder of a religious house was residence there. In this way royal palaces grew up at Holyrood Abbey and at Dunfermline. The palace at Dunfermline was a favourite residence of Anne, queen of James VI. Here several of her children were born, including her second son, who was to become Charles I of Scotland and England in 1625.

After his departure for England in 1603, Charles was to return only once to the country of his birth, for his coronation at the Palace of Holyroodhouse in Edinburgh in 1633. Here he caused offence by being crowned according to the *English* rather than the Scottish ritual. The king is seen here in a classic pose.

The king tried to return to Scotland once more, this time at the head of a military force in 1639, but the Covenanting Army prevented him getting further than Berwick-upon-Tweed.

The abbey church, in the background, rises above the palace in the foreground.

ST MARY'S CHURCH, GRANDTULLY

Sir William Steuart
(1566/7–c 1646)

This low, white-washed building at Grandtully might be a row of cottages: it is in fact a church. Originally erected in about 1533, Grandtully's repair in 1636 is most eloquently attested. Inside, a fine painted ceiling covers about a third of the vault. It bears the arms of the owner, Sir William Steuart, 11th Laird of Grandtully (shown here), and his wife, Dame Agnes Moncreiff, as well as those of the local nobility and biblical scenes. The richness of the interior decoration renders Grandtully a fine example of church planning and furnishings around the time of King Charles I's homecoming in 1633. This homecoming was less than successful, not only because Charles was crowned according to the English rite, but also because he made clear his dislike of the informal manners of his Scottish nobles.

CRAIGMILLAR CASTLE

Sir John Gilmour (1605–71)

In 1660 Sir John Gilmour, Lord President of the Court of Session, purchased Craigmillar Castle from George Preston. The Prestons had acquired the estate in 1374 and erected the tower and enclosure wall, which also protected ranges of rooms in the courtyard. Sir Simon Preston received Mary Queen of Scots at Craigmillar in 1563 and 1566 and served three terms as Provost of Edinburgh during the queen's reign.

Sir John Gilmour was a member of the new middle class that developed in Scotland during the seventeenth century. A lawyer, he was a royalist during the Civil War, and was rewarded by

appointment as Lord President of the Court of Session in 1661 after the restoration of Charles II. He undertook extensive building at Craigmillar, but the family abandoned the castle 100 years later, moving to nearby Inch House. By 1775 the castle was a ruin.

Craigmillar has given its name to an extensive area across south Edinburgh, and is retained in the title of the present head of the family, Sir Ian Gilmour of Gilmerton and Craigmillar, a Minister in Margaret Thatcher's first administration.

FORT CHARLOTTE, LERWICK

Charles II (king 1660–85)
John Paul Jones (1747–92)

Between 1650 and 1677, England and Scotland fought three wars against the Dutch, largely for commercial reasons. During the second Dutch War of 1665–7, a fort was erected overlooking the Sound of Bressay in Shetland in order to protect the anchorage.

The fort was planned by Robert Mylne, master-mason to King Charles II. It is roughly pentagonal with a battery overlooking the Sound. Inside was placed a barrack-block for 100 men commanded by Colonel Sinclair. The Dutch did indeed attack Shetland in 1667, but by that time the fort was garrisoned by 1000 men and armed with 40 guns: the Dutch withdrew. The fort was abandoned and six years later burnt by the Dutch in the next war.

Ironically, this medal was struck at Scheveningen in the Netherlands in 1660 to celebrate the Restoration: Charles had spent most of his exile there.

Fort Charlotte was rebuilt in the 1780s during the American War of Independence as a defence against raids by American privateers led by John Paul Jones, who was born in Kirkcudbright. Jones is seen here in a copy of the 1780 bust by Jean Antoine Houdon, made to commemorate his attack on Leith and subsequent victory off Flamborough Head. The fort contained a house for the commanding officer, officers' quarters, barracks, a kitchen and mess, magazine and ammunition store. However, its military use did not survive long into the nineteenth century once the need for fort's construction had passed.

Above left: medal of Charles II; above right: bust of John Paul Jones.

HOLYROOD ABBEY

James VII
(1633–1701; reigned 1685–8/9)

It could be claimed that the man who more than anyone is responsible for the destruction of the Abbey of Holyrood is King James VII of Scotland, II of England. James inherited the crown from his brother Charles II and, in spite of his Roman Catholicism, enjoyed popularity during the early part of his reign. However, the birth of a son and heir in 1688 – and the possibility of the establishment of a Roman Catholic dynasty – produced a strong reaction. James' son-in-law, William III of Orange, crossed to Britain at the invitation of a group of English Protestant nobles, and James fled.

James VII is unusual in that he had previously lived in Scotland. From 1679 to 1682 he had lived at the Palace of Holyroodhouse as the High Commissioner of his brother Charles II. In reality, he had been exiled to Scotland when London got too hot for him. When he became king he re-established the abbey church of Holyrood as a chapel royal and as a home for the Knights of the Thistle. The existing congregation built a new church on the Canongate, which survives to this day. The new chapel royal, however, so excited the wrath of the Edinburgh mob that they sacked and burnt it in 1688 and thus perished one of Scotland's greatest monasteries – and another foundation of David I.

Sir Peter Lely's portrait depicts James when Duke of York.

CLAYPOTTS CASTLE

John Graham of Claverhouse
(1649?–89)

Claypotts was built by John Strachan, whose initials and arms appear on a skewput together with the dates 1569 and 1588 (and whose will survives dated 1593). The plan is in the form of a central rectangular block with round towers attached to opposite corners. Approach to the castle was well protected by shot-holes, though by this time comfort was more important than defence.

In 1620 the estate was bought by Sir William Graham of Claverhouse. His great-grandson, John, was elevated to the peerage by King James VII and II as Viscount Dundee in 1688. In the following year he led the Jacobite forces at the Battle of Killiecrankie, in support of his now-exiled king. Although Dundee won the battle, he lost his life in the process, and the Jacobite Uprising collapsed as a result. Claypotts was forfeited to the Crown and came into the hands of the Douglas family. It is still owned by the Douglas-Home family.

Ink drawing of John Graham by David Paton.

DUFF
HOUSE

William Adam (1688–1748)

In May 1735 William Duff gave William Adam, illustrated here, a commission to build a new house at Banff. The result was the erection of Duff House, the grandest eighteenth-century house in the north of Scotland.

Both Adam and Duff were new men. Adam had risen from mason through land surveyor to architect. He had worked on other great houses, but at Duff House he was starting a new building and he planned a great baroque masterpiece in the classical style. William Duff was a dealer in land bonds on the basis of which he built up a great estate. Duff House was to be built to consolidate his new position in society: as his house was being created, he rose through the peerage from Lord Braco to Earl Fife.

The foundation stone was laid on 11 June 1735, but by October the first difference between patron and client occurred and relations deteriorated. Work stopped in 1741 and a subsequent court case was only determined in 1748, in favour of Adam. As a result the interior was left undecorated until the succession of the 2nd Earl Fife in 1763. Even so, only the main block was completed. One wing was added in 1870, though this was demolished after bomb damage in 1942.

Duff House was opened in 1995 as an outpost of the National Galleries of Scotland.

HUNTINGTOWER

Sir George Murray (1694–1760)

Situated to the west of Perth, Huntingtower was built by the Ruthven family. The Ruthvens had a chequered history, being involved in several unsavoury episodes, such as helping in the murder of David Riccio at the Palace of Holyroodhouse in 1566, forcing Mary Queen of Scots to abdicate, and attempting a *coup d'état* against her son, James VI. The last members of the family were executed for an alleged plot against the king in 1600.

Sixty years later, Huntingtower was granted to James Murray, Earl of Tullibardine. The Murrays were – indeed are – one of Scotland's great families. Its several branches trace their descent from Freskin, who established himself first in West Lothian and then in Moray during the reign of David I. The Bothwell branch were strong supporters of Scottish independence, fighting with Wallace and Bruce, and died out as a result.

The 6th Earl of Tullibardine was created Duke of Atholl. It was at Huntingtower on 4 October 1694 that his wife, Katherine, gave birth to their fourth son George. The heir to the dukedom, William, as well as George was 'out' in the Jacobite Uprisings of 1715, 1719 and 1745. The best of the Jacobite generals, Lord George was Lieutenant-General of the Jacobite army, but out of favour with Prince Charles Edward in the days before Culloden. He did not support the site chosen for the battle, but fought bravely and was among the last to leave the field. He died in exile in 1760. His son succeeded to the dukedom in 1764.

RUTHVEN BARRACKS

Major-General George Wade (1673–1748)

George Wade, son of an Irishman who had served in Cromwell's army, rose from ensign to field-marshal in the British army during a career that spanned 55 years. He also served his country in an entirely different manner, being MP for Bath from 1722 until his death in 1748.

Between the Jacobite Uprisings of '15 and the '45 Wade supervised the building of 250 miles (400 km) of roads and about 40 bridges in the Highlands. These roads, including that over the Corrieyairack Pass shown in the portrait, improved access between the government's forts and barracks. One such barracks was at Ruthven. Built between 1719 and 1721 on the site of a Comyn castle, its garrison was 120 strong. In 1734 it was extended by Wade who ordered the construction of a stable-block for 30 horses (the outlying building to the left).

Ironically, Wade's roads aided the advance of the Jacobite army in 1745, while Wade himself was isolated in Newcastle by the poor roads across northern England. Ruthven was captured by the Jacobites and served as their last rallying point after their defeat at Culloden on 16 April 1746.

DUNSTAFFNAGE
CASTLE

Flora Macdonald (1722–90)

The escape of Prince Charles Edward Stuart, 'Bonnie Prince Charlie', from Scotland after his defeat at the Battle of Culloden on 16 April 1746 is forever linked with the name of Flora Macdonald.

Flora Macdonald was born in South Uist, but moved to Skye, then completed her education in Edinburgh. She was on a visit to Benbecula when Prince Charles Edward arrived and she helped him to escape to Skye disguised as an Irish spinning maid, Betty Burke. Although the prince escaped, Flora was arrested and briefly imprisoned in the Campbell castle of Dunstaffnage before being sent to the Tower of London. Freed by the Act of Indemnity in 1747, the same year in which this portrait by Richard Wilson was painted, she was fêted in London before returning to Scotland. Flora Macdonald married, farmed in Skye for the rest of her life, apart from a brief period in North Carolina, and died in Skye.

Dunstaffnage Castle had been erected by the MacDougalls in the thirteenth century, and although it first came into the hands of the Campbells in 1321 or 1322, it was another 150 years before it became permanently theirs. It is held today by the Captain of Dunstaffnage on behalf of the Duke of Argyll.

DUN BEAG
BROCH

Samuel Johnson (1709–85) and
James Boswell (1740–95)

During the eighteenth century several people visited the Highlands and Islands of Scotland and recorded their experiences. One of the most famous visits was by the English writer Samuel Johnson and the Scottish writer James Boswell in 1773, when they undertook a tour of the Western Isles lasting three months. Each wrote and published his own account of the journey. Johnson's book was entitled *Journey to the Western Isles* and was published first, in 1773. Boswell's *Journal of a Tour to the Hebrides with Samuel Johnson LL.D* appeared in 1786, nine months after the death of Johnson, and was to be the first part of his famous *Life of Johnson*.

On Skye they met Flora Macdonald and stayed at Dunvegan Castle, seat of the Macleods. On 21 September, while travelling between Dunvegan and Ullinish, they visited Dun Beag and in his account of the journey Johnson published a detailed description of the building, including measurements (42 feet in diameter and 9 feet high), and offered speculation about its original state and how it had been constructed. He considered its date, which he acknowledged was unknown, and function: he doubted that it was a fortress but suggested that its purpose was to protect sheep and cattle at night. In short, Johnson furnished a model and concise archaeological description and interpretation of the ancient dwelling. In one area we can do better: this was not a Danish fort, as suggested by one of his party, but a dwelling erected some centuries before in the Iron Age.

Johnson ends his account with a comment which might serve as a mission statement for Historic Scotland: 'edifices, either standing or ruined, are the chief records of an illiterate nation'.

Far left: James Boswell painted by George Willison in 1765. Left: Samuel Johnson by James Barry about 1777.

87

HOLYROOD PARK

James Hutton (1726–97)

In the centre of Edinburgh lies a royal park, Holyrood. Over the centuries the park has seen many events, and has been used for many purposes. Surprisingly, this includes several industrial activities, such as quarrying.

The hard rock was particularly useful as building stone and was used to pave London streets. Salisbury Crags owe their present distinctive outline to the quarrying there from at least the seventeenth century. By the nineteenth century the scale of quarrying began to alarm the citizens of Edinburgh and in 1831 the House of Lords ruled that it should stop.

The exposed quarry face was studied by geologists interested in determining the age of the earth. One of these was James Hutton. He was of the opinion that the rocks were volcanic in origin. He asked quarrymen to preserve a particular piece of rock which exhibited a vein of iron ore. This is known as Hutton's Rock to this day.

Hutton's Rock, illustrated above, is a suitable memorial to the man who has been called the father of modern geology. It is also appropriately placed for Hutton was an Edinburgh man, though he spent most of his adult life on his family farm outside the city where he wrote his most important papers. His *Theory of the Earth*, delivered in Edinburgh in 1785 and subsequently published, argued that heat was an important agent in altering the earth through volcanic activity and lifting land.

CASTLE HILL
TRIG POINT

William Roy (1726–90)

In 1747 William Roy, Assistant Quartermaster in North Britain, born at Miltonhead, near Carluke in Lanarkshire, 21 years before, was given the task of preparing a map of the Highlands in order to assist in its pacification following the Uprising of 1745–6.

The mapping of the Highlands took six years, after which the team moved on to southern Scotland. It was during these latter years, 1752–5, that Roy's interest in the Romans was first evidenced. His earliest known plan of an archaeological site is the Roman fort now known

as Netherby. He went on to draw all the major sites of Scotland, including Birrens, Burnswark, Ardoch and the Antonine Wall. Roy's *Military Antiquities of the Romans in North Britain* was published posthumously in 1793. His map of Roman Britain was not surpassed until 1924.

Roy joined the army in 1755 and had a long and successful career. In 1763 he proposed a national survey as an aid to the defence of the country. It was to be 20 years before the first practical steps were taken, the laying out of the first great surveying triangle. In 1791, 11 months after Roy's death, it was determined to create 'A General Survey of the Kingdom ... under the direction of the Master General of the Ordnance'. The triangulation continued and 'trig' points were established across the kingdom. This particular trig point is on the former Iron Age hill fort, Castle Hill, next to the Antonine Wall which Roy surveyed.

Left: Paul Sandby drew Roy's surveyors at work beside Loch Rannoch in 1749. One soldier uses a theodolite, while two measure with a chain between the fore and back stations marked by flags.

TRINITY HOUSE

Admiral Duncan (1731–1804)

Hidden in Leith, on the north side of Edinburgh, is a building reflecting a long history, Trinity House. Its foundation stone was laid on 4 June 1816, the work being completed two years later. Yet, the body for which the building was erected, the Corporation of the Masters and Assistants of the Trinity House of Leith, is of greater antiquity. It had erected a hospital on the site in 1555, still recorded on a date stone. The origins of the Corporation were even earlier, perhaps as long ago as 1380.

From at least the 16th century the Corporation was allowed to impose a levy on goods passing through the port of Leith. These and other funds raised from shipping were used to succour the poor and needy. To these duties was added the piloting of ships in the Firth of Forth. Naturally, the Masters of Trinity House have over the centuries also been concerned with the provision of lighthouses and harbours in the Forth. Such matters have, at times, dragged them into affairs of state.

In 1797 Trinity House pilots helped Admiral Duncan's ships navigate the Forth and after his victory over the Dutch at the Battle of Camperdown they gave him the Freedom of the Corporation. His portrait by Henry Raeburn still hangs in Trinity House.

BELL MILL, STANLEY MILLS

Sir Richard Arkwright (1732–92)

Arkwright was born at Preston in Lancashire and started his working life as a wig-maker. Through his work he became interested in the manufacture of textiles. He patented his first spinning machine in 1769. He and his business partners subsequently established factories at Cromford and Nottingham.

In 1785 Arkwright went into business in Scotland, building a factory for the manufacture of cotton on the River Tay at Stanley. The five-storey Bell Mill, seen here, was completed in 1790 and is a fine building in a classical style. The factory was expanded on several occasions during the nineteenth century and continued in operation into the 1980s.

Richard Arkwright's genius lay in recognising the advantages of other inventions and combining them in newer and better machinery. He also changed the way industry was organised by combining all the processes of textile manufacturing from carding to spinning in the one factory: previously, the different processes had been undertaken separately, mostly in the home. This, together with his business acumen, brought him a considerable fortune and a knighthood.

KINNEIL COTTAGE

James Watt (1736–1819)

James Watt was born and educated at Greenock. In 1763, while employed by Glasgow University as an instrument maker, he was asked to repair one of Newcomen's steam engines. While working on the machine, Watt realised that he could improve it. The physical realisation of his theories, however, proved harder to effect. Finance was one problem, but in addition Watt was a perfectionist and the equipment was not yet available to build the machine that he wanted to produce. Help with the former came from John Roebuck, founder of the Carron Ironworks near Falkirk. He provided a laboratory in the form of a cottage on his estate at Kinneil near Bo'ness on the Forth. Here Watt built a full-sized experimental engine, part of which still survives outside the now roofless cottage. Finance continued to plague him and forced him to undertake work surveying canals, including the Forth and Clyde Canal and the Crinan Canal. His financial problems were solved in 1774 when he moved to Birmingham and went into partnership with Matthew Boulton. Furthermore, technology now caught up with Watt's ideas and he was able to build a steam engine in 1776, which trebled the power of the Newcomen engine.

Watt had many other inventions to his credit, all of which made significant contributions to the Industrial Revolution. He continued to invent until his retirement in 1800, after which he maintained his interest through a workshop at his home. His business was continued by his son, also James Watt.

DRYBURGH ABBEY

David Erskine,
11th Earl of Buchan (1742–1829)

Buchan in 1780 founded the Society of Antiquaries of Scotland, the second oldest archaeological society in the British Isles, and the oldest learned society in Scotland. A man of volatile temper, he soon parted from the Society. In 1786 Buchan, a descendant of the sixteenth-century commendators of Dryburgh, bought the abbey and set up his home at Dryburgh House where he lived until his death over 40 years later.

Buchan bought the abbey ruins to ensure their survival, and he explored them through excavations. He used them as a sort of ornament in his magnificent gardens. Among his adornments was an obelisk erected beside the gatehouse to mark the foundation of the abbey by Hugh de Moreville in 1150, and a statue of William Wallace on the hill overlooking the abbey. Buchan's deathmask survives on his tomb in the cloisters.

De Moreville had been the constable of King David I and he established the abbey here in 1150 for Premonstratensians or 'White' Canons. He later joined the abbey where he died, a novice, in 1162. In turn, Buchan was buried here in the sacristy. Three years later, Sir Walter Scott was laid to rest in the north transept.

Today, the ruins of the abbey founded by de Moreville, protected and beautified by Buchan, are among the most graceful in Scotland.

CARDONESS CASTLE

Robert Burns (1759–96)

The McCullochs acquired the estate of Cardoness and built the castle in the late fifteenth century. They were a particularly troublesome family, in nearly continuous feud with their neighbours. The last of the line to be associated with Cardoness was Godfrey McCulloch. The McCullochs lost their estates, including the castle, in 1628. However, they continued to harass the new owners until Godfrey shot and killed John Gordon, the new owner. He fled abroad, but was recognised on his return. He gained the dubious distinction of being one of the last to be executed by 'The Maiden', the guillotine in Edinburgh.

Cardoness thereafter fell into disrepair. Like so many places in south-west Scotland, it appeared in a Robert Burns poem, in this case *Election Ballads*:

'Sae in the tower o' Cardoness
A howlet sits at noon'

The Maiden guillotine, now in the Museum of Scotland, Edinburgh (bottom right).

thus bearing witness to the fate met by so many of the buildings featured in this book.

This portrait of Burns was painted in 1787 by Alexander Nasmyth.

MELROSE ABBEY

Sir Walter Scott (1771–1832)

'If though would'st view fair Melrose aright, go visit it by the pale moonlight.' So wrote Sir Walter Scott, though he had to admit that, 'I had been guilty of sending persons a bat-hunting to see the ruins of Melrose by moonlight which I never saw myself.'

Melrose is one of the most beautiful abbeys in Scotland, but it saw much fighting during its life. The kirk, one of the glories of medieval church architecture, was erected following the sacking of the abbey by the army of Richard II of England in 1385, who then helped to pay for the rebuilding, which was, unfortunately, never finished. An inscription in the south transept records work by the French master-mason Jean Morrow, who also worked at Glasgow, Paisley, Nithsdale (presumably Lincluden) and Galloway.

Scott copied many of the details from Melrose in his house at Abbotsford, a building which is the physical manifestation of the great writer and his works. Scott was the inventor of the historical novel and many of Scotland's ruins and historic buildings feature in his books. In one case, a site has come to be known by Scott's name for it, Jarlshof in Shetland.

Sir William Allan's portrait, appropriately, places Scott in a rural setting.

SMAILHOLM TOWER

J M W Turner (1775–1851)

Inspired by Sir Walter Scott's vision, artists came to the Borders to record the landscape and its historic buildings through their paintings. One such artist was J M W Turner. Turner came to Scotland on four occasions. In 1822 he witnessed the visit of King George IV. Returning in 1831, he stayed five days with Scott at Abbotsford, visiting many places, including Smailholm. The connection between the two men extended to business affairs for Turner illustrated some of Scott's books.

There can be no better illustration of the interplay between poet and painter than Turner's depiction of the young Walter Scott and his Aunt Janet at Smailholm painted shortly before Scott's death in 1832. Turner's painting was an acknowledgement of this vital link between the great writer and his past.

Walter Scott, through his writing, encouraged people to look at the Scottish countryside in a different way. Where previously only barrenness had been seen, now the hills and valleys were valued in their own right. Scott peopled the countryside with his heroes – and villains – and with mythical and magical figures.

As a child, Walter had been sent to recuperate from illness at his grandfather's farm at Sandyknowe, in the shadow of the ruined Smailholm Tower. Here his imagination was fired by his aunt's stories.

INNOCENT RAILWAY

James Jardine (1776–1858)

This tunnel on the Innocent Railway in Edinburgh is one of the earliest in the world. Opened in 1831, the railway was created to take coal from Dalkeith to Edinburgh. But it soon became popular with the public and, for a time, carried passengers as well. The line acquired its unusual name because it was horse-drawn at a time when steam engines were still considered dangerous. The line was converted to steam in 1845.

The engineer for the line, which ran for 9 miles (14.4 km), was James Jardine. The stone for the tunnel was quarried at Craigleith in Edinburgh. The tunnel is 566 yards (524 m) long, 20 feet (6 m) wide and 15 feet (4.5 m) high with a gradient of 1 in 30. The railway was closed in 1968 and the part of the route which runs through Holyrood Park serves as a cycle-way today.

ELGIN
CATHEDRAL

Robert Reid (1774–1856)

Elgin is one of Scotland's great medieval cathedrals. It is not surprising therefore that it was one of the monuments protected by Robert Reid during the brief life of the Office of Works for Scotland from 1827 to 1831. Reid, an Edinburgh man, had been appointed King's Architect and Surveyor in Scotland in 1809, and he was a natural choice to head the new Scottish Office of Works. Here he was not entirely his own man for he was responsible to the quaintly named Barons of the Exchequer.

As head of the Office of Works, Reid had in his care, not only public buildings, but several ruins as well. These included the remains of several of the medieval cathedrals of Scotland, which had fallen to the Crown after the Reformation of 1560 and the abolition of episcopacy in 1689. Reid worked on Arbroath Abbey, Elgin Cathedral and Fortrose Cathedral and was also involved at Glasgow Cathedral and St Andrews.

Reid can fairly claim to have helped lay the foundation for modern methods of consolidating ruins for in 1829 he wrote, 'restoration should not be the object, but that repairs, on such decayed and ancient edifices ... should be executed for ... their preservation and ... the less appearance of interference with their present state and construction the better'.

LONGMORE HOSPITAL

Sir James Simpson (1811–70)

Two great advances in the nineteenth century aided the survival of patients and caused significant changes to the organisation of the medical world: chloroform and antiseptics. James Young Simpson (right) was responsible for the former and Joseph Lister for the latter. These discoveries allowed more successful operations to be undertaken and created a need for more hospitals to be built. One such hospital was Longmore Hospital on Salisbury Place in Edinburgh, now the headquarters of Historic Scotland.

The hospital owed its existence to a bequest by John Longmore, an Edinburgh solicitor. The money was donated to the Edinburgh Association for the Relief of Incurables, which had bought 8 Salisbury Place, opening it as a hospital in 1875. The bequest of £10,000 and an annual income of £300 allowed the Association to buy 9 and 10 Salisbury Place. They were replaced by a new hospital, designed by the architect M Dick Peddie, which opened on 10 December 1880.

The hospital was extended on three occasions before the end of the century. This involved the demolition of

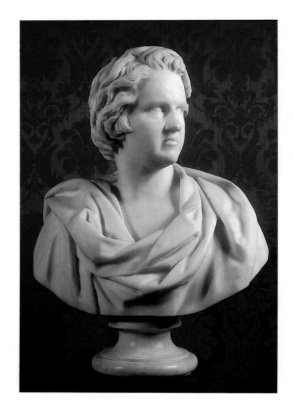

the entire row of villas along the north side of Salisbury Place, including a school, Wilson's Academy.

Until 1948 the hospital was heavily dependent on donations to survive and the donors' names were inscribed on boards that still survive in the present building. The hospital closed in 1991; three years later it became the headquarters of Historic Scotland.

DIRLETON CASTLE GARDENS

David Thomson (1823–1909)

David Thomson was born at Torliosk on the Isle of Mull. He left home at the age of 14 to work first in the gardens of Corsairs House in Lanarkshire and then at Bothwell Castle where the head gardener was Andrew Turnbull, the most famous plant grower of his day. From 1844 to 1858 Thomson worked in England, including at Kew Gardens, and he published his first article.

David Thomson returned to Scotland in 1858 to become head gardener at Archerfield House in East Lothian, a post he held for 10 years before moving on to Drumlanrig. The Archerfield estate included Dirleton Castle and there Thomson tended and developed the gardens.

The gardens at Dirleton had already been partly laid out before Thomson arrived but he brought them to a state of magnificence that won wide acclaim. The gardens were laid out in geometrical patterns and planted with colourful flowers. Recent advances in flower breeding allowed a wide variety of bright colours to be displayed. Thomson was clearly skilled at both propagating plants and laying out the gardens and his work was justly admired.

Thomson wrote several books on gardening, including *The Handy Book of the Flower Garden* in 1868 while he was at Dirleton Castle.

Different ideas about gardens led to changes at Dirleton in the 1920s such as the planting of the herbaceous borders, which have brought Dirleton Castle gardens into the *Guinness Book of Records* as the longest such border in the world. The west garden, developed by David Thomson, was restored in 1993 after archaeological investigation and using earlier plans and notes.

DUN
CARLOWAY

General Augustus
Henry Pitt-Rivers (1827–1900)

On 18 August 1882 Queen Victoria signed an Act for the better protection of Ancient Monuments, the first piece of conservation legislation to be passed by a British government. This allowed for the appointment of an Inspector of Ancient Monuments. On 1 January 1883, the first Inspector took up his appointment, Augustus Henry Pitt-Rivers, a gentleman archaeologist, at a salary of £250 a year.

The Act protected 50 monuments in Britain, including 21 in Scotland, and allowed for them to be brought into State care. Among the first to come into care were those offered by Sir Herbert Maxwell, an important landowner in Galloway and a distinguished antiquarian (he was later President of the Society of Antiquaries of Scotland and Chairman of the Royal Commission on the Ancient and Historical Monuments of Scotland).

Pitt-Rivers was very energetic in the pursuit of his duties, travelling the length and breadth of Britain inspecting monuments. He was in Scotland nearly every year from 1883 to 1890. In 1885 he visited the broch known as Dun Carloway in the Western Isles and made a drawing of it. The broch was taken into State care in 1887.

Pitt-Rivers gave up his salary in 1890, but continued as honorary Inspector until his death in 1900. By that time he had brought 43 monuments into State care, forming the basis of the present portfolio.

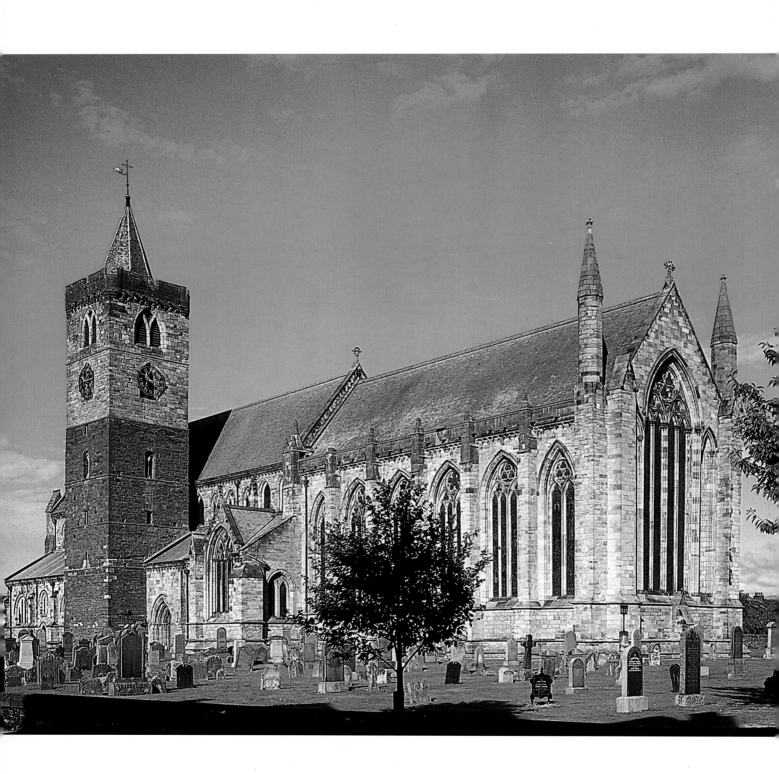

DUNBLANE CATHEDRAL

Sir Rowand Anderson (1834–1921)

David I established a bishopric at Dunblane and the lower storeys of the tower date from this time. In the mid-thirteenth century the church was rebuilt by Bishop Clement (d 1258). After the Reformation in 1560 the Protestant Church had no need for such a large building and Dunblane was left in a state of disrepair: within 40 years the roof of the nave fell in.

In the late nineteenth century Mrs Wallace of Glassingall donated the money for the repair of the nave. The work was put into the hands of Sir Rowand Anderson, one of Scotland's leading architects. The roof was replaced, the window tracery, which had suffered from erosion, was carefully renewed and the windows were reglazed. Anderson designed the screen between the nave and the choir, while shortly before and after World War II Sir Robert Lorimer designed the choir stalls, organ case, reredos screen and the pews. Thus was Dunblane Cathedral brought back to something approaching its former magnificence.

W Graham Bell prepared this pencil drawing for Anderson's inclusion in the windows of the Findley Building in Queen Street, Edinburgh, opened in 1890 as the new home of the Scottish National Portrait Gallery and the Society of Antiquaries of Scotland.

STIRLING BRIDGE

Robert Louis Stevenson (1850–94)

'The bridge is close under the castle hill, an old, high, narrow bridge with pinnacles along the parapet.' Thus R L Stevenson described Stirling Bridge in *Kidnapped*

when his two heroes, David Balfour and Allan Breck Stewart, came from the north side and attempted to cross. Before the challenge of the guard, they retreated eastwards, eventually crossing at Limekilns.

Kidnapped is set in 1751, in the aftermath of the 1745 Uprising, and it is appropriate that the bridge appears in the novel for it was damaged as a result of that Uprising. The government forces blew up the southern arch to prevent the Jacobite army entering the town of Stirling; it was repaired in 1749.

Today, the Wallace Monument overlooks the bridge from Abbey Crag. Financed by public subscription, the monument was built between 1859 and 1869.

Stevenson was born in Edinburgh but died in Tahiti, where many of his best books were written, drawing on his earlier experiences in Scotland. He looks every inch the story-teller in this portrait by Count Girolamo Nerli painted only two years before his death.

SKARA BRAE

Professor Vere Gordon Childe
(1892–1957)

Skara Brae on Orkney is a prehistoric village which was occupied from about 3000–2500 BC. It came to light after a great storm in 1850 and is one of the most interesting and famous sites of this period in Europe.

Gordon Childe was born in Sydney in Australia. He moved to Britain in 1914 and graduated from Oxford two years later. A spell as private secretary to the Prime Minister of New South Wales was short-lived before his interest in archaeology took over. He travelled in Eastern and Central Europe and worked in London before becoming the first holder of the new Professorship in Archaeology in the University of Edinburgh, endowed by the 7th and last Baron Abercromby of Aboukir in 1927.

Childe was a dedicated scholar and a prolific writer, seeking to extend knowledge of archaeology to as wide an audience as possible. Many of his books, such as *The Dawn of European Civilisation* (1925), although overtaken by increased knowledge, remain classic treatments of the subject and are influential even today.

Childe was of the view that British prehistory could only be understood in its international context. While in Scotland, he excavated extensively in the Lowlands, Highlands and Islands, including at Skara Brae, where he is seen above.

After nearly 20 years in Scotland, Childe moved to London where he became Director of the Institute of Archaeology. In 1956 he retired and returned to Australia. Here, fearing the gradual loss of his faculties, he committed suicide by walking off a cliff in the Blue Mountains on 19 October 1957.

A R N O L BLACKHOUSE

Mr and Mrs David Macleod

Arnol Blackhouse is one of the youngest monuments in State care in Scotland, being built less than 100 years before it was taken into care in 1965. At that time three generations of the family lived in the house, the grandmother being the daughter of the builder of the house, Mr David Macleod (seen left with his wife). Today, his great granddaughter, Mrs Chrisetta Smith, is the custodian of the site.

Arnol Blackhouse was built by a crofter as a dwelling and farm house. The main building was divided into two roughly equal parts by the entrance, the bedroom and living room lying to one side and the byre the other. The house shared a party wall with the barn: the south wall of the barn was rebuilt following the nearby explosion of a land-mine about 1940. Beside the building lay the stackyard.

The living room had a central hearth where a peat fire burned constantly: the peats were cut in the autumn and stacked outside the house to dry. Heat was also provided by the cattle in the byre at the other end of the building.

Each crofter grew his or her own food – mostly oats, potatoes, turnips and cabbages. While much of the processing of corn was undertaken domestically, there were at least four corn-drying kilns in Arnol for larger scale work. In 1960 the stock at this blackhouse consisted of a cow and a calf, 17 sheep, 20 poultry and 6 chickens. The family income was supplemented by fishing, weaving, and service in the Merchant Navy, which sometimes resulted in the appearance of exotic items in the crofts of the Western Isles.

A typical blackhouse had walls of double thickness for insulation and a thatched roof. The peat stack stands in the foreground.

FURTHER READING

The Batsford/Historic Scotland series of books provides further information about many of the monuments and buildings featured in this book. They include:

Ian Armit, *Celtic Scotland*, 2000.
P J Ashmore, *Neolithic and Bronze Age Scotland*, 2000.
D J Breeze, *Roman Scotland, Frontier Country*, 2000.
D J Breeze, *Historic Scotland*, 1999.
R Fawcett, *Scottish Abbeys and Priories*, 2000.
R Fawcett, *Scottish Cathedrals*, 1997.
R Fawcett, *Stirling Castle*, 1995.
Sally Foster, *Picts, Gaels and Scots*, 2000.
Brian Lavery, *Maritime Scotland*, 2001.
Iain MacIvor, *Edinburgh Castle*, 1997.
Colin Martin, *Scotland's Historic Shipwrecks*, 1999.
Anna Ritchie, *Iona*, 1997.
Anna Ritchie, *Viking Scotland*, 2000.
Anna Ritchie, *Prehistoric Orkney*, 2001.
C J Tabraham, *Scotland's Castles*, 2000.
C J Tabraham and Doreen Grove, *Fortress Scotland and the Jacobites*, 2001.
Val Turner, *Ancient Shetland*, 1998.
Caroline Wickham-Jones, *Scotland's First Settlers*, 2000.
Peter Yeoman, *Medieval Scotland*, 1997.
Peter Yeoman, *Scottish Medieval Pilgrimages*, 1999.

From Historic Scotland:
David J Breeze, *A Queen's Progress*, 1987.
Richard Fawcett, *Scottish Medieval Churches*, 1984.
Anna Ritchie, *Scotland BC*, 1988.
Anna Ritchie, *Picts*, 1989.
Anna Ritchie and David J Breeze, *Invaders of Scotland*, 1991.
Christopher Tabraham, *Scottish Castles and Fortifications*, 1986.

For a general history of Scotland, Michael Lynch's *Scotland, A New History* (Edinburgh 1995) can be recommended. *A History Book for Scots*, by Walter Bower, edited by D E R Watts (Edinburgh 1998), offers an abridged version of the *Scotichronicon*.

ACKNOWLEDGEMENTS

 I am grateful to my colleagues Josephine Barry, Richard Fawcett, Sally Foster, Doreen Grove, Chris Tabraham and Pam Wood for their advice; to Jackie Henrie for her rigorous proof-reading, and to David Henrie of Historic Scotland's Photographic Unit who took photographs for this book. I should also like to thank Deborah Hunter of the National Galleries of Scotland for her assistance. I am also grateful to the following bodies for permission to reproduce a wide range of images: Her Majesty The Queen (page 40); Blair Museum (page 42); the British Library (page 90); Corpus Christi College, Cambridge (page 38); Dennis Coutts (page 24); Sir Ian Gilmour (page 71); His Grace the Duke of Hamilton (page 49); Hunterian Museum and Art Gallery (page 11); The National Galleries of Scotland (pages 46, 51, 52, 54, 56, 67, 73, 74, 76, 79, 80, 82, 84, 86, 88, 97, 98, 100, 103, 107, 108, 110, 117 and 119); The National Library of Scotland (page 26); The National Museums of Scotland (pages 13, 35, 37, 98 and 100); The National Portrait Gallery, London (pages 86, 95, 105); Norwegian National Archives (page 28); Antonia Reeve Photography (page 92); Pitt Rivers Museum, Oxford (page 114); the Royal Shakespeare Company (page 22); His Grace the Duke of Roxburghe (page 26); Vassar College Art Gallery, Poughkeepsie, New York (gift of Matthew Vassar, 1864) (page 104).

FRIENDS OF HISTORIC SCOTLAND

Membership of the Friends' organisation gives free admission to over 300 Historic Scotland sites; half-price admission to English Heritage, Welsh Cadw and Manx National Heritage sites in the first year and free entry thereafter, a free sites directory, full-colour quarterly magazine and other benefits; plus the satisfaction of contributing to the preservation of Scotland's built heritage for future generations. For further information write to Historic Scotland, Longmore House, Salisbury Place, Edinburgh EH9 1SH or tel 0131 668 8600 (Main), 0131 668 8999 (Friends). Details of all properties can be found on www.historicscotland.gov.uk

PRACTICAL INFORMATION

Access to most of the 300 and more monuments in the care of Historic Scotland is free. At less than 70 of them there is an entry charge. From April to September, sites for which there is a charge are open every day, Monday–Sunday, 9.30am–6.30pm. From October to March restricted openings apply and some properties close completely; opening hours are normally Mon–Sat 9.30am–4.30pm, with some open 2.00–4.30pm on Sunday. The last ticket is sold 30 minutes before closing (45 minutes at Edinburgh, Stirling and Urquhart Castles and at Fort George). Monuments with special opening times are listed below.

Some monuments, in particular those on islands, can be difficult of access and visitors are recommended to consult the local tourist information office or the Historic Scotland guidebook.

The photographs in this book are available from Historic Scotland, Photographic Library or by telephone 0131 668 8647. Guidebooks (and a catalogue) to many of the monuments are also available from Historic Scotland at the address above.

Aberdour Castle Closed Thursday afternoons and Fridays in winter

Arnol Blackhouse Closed Sundays

Blackness Castle Closed Thursday afternoons and Fridays in winter

Cambuskenneth Abbey Open summer only

Cardoness Castle Open weekends only in winter

Castle Campbell Closed Thursday afternoons, Fridays and Sunday mornings in winter

Claypotts Castle Limited opening: tel 01786 431 324

Craigmillar Castle Closed Thursday afternoons and Fridays in winter

Crichton Castle Open summer only

Duff House Open all summer from 10.00am to 5.00pm. Open Thursday to Sunday in winter 10.00am to 5.00pm

Dunblane Cathedral Open on Sundays from 1.30pm

Dundonald Castle Open 7 days a week from April to October 10.00am to 5.00pm

Dundrennan Abbey Open all summer and weekends in winter

Dunfermline Palace Closed Thursday afternoons and Fridays in winter

Dunstaffnage Castle Closed Thursdays and Fridays in winter. Sunday mornings open 9am all year

Edinburgh Castle Open all year 7 days a week April to September 9.30am to 6.00pm October to March 9.30am to 5.00pm. Last ticket sold 45 minutes before closing

Elgin Cathedral Closed Thursday afternoons and Fridays in winter

Gurness Broch Open summer only. Joint entry ticket for all Orkney staffed monuments

Holyrood Abbey Access only through the Palace on payment of a charge

Huntingtower Closed Thursday afternoons and Fridays in winter

Huntly Castle Closed Thursday afternoons and Fridays in winter

Inchcolm Abbey Open summer only. Additional charge for ferry trip. Tel 0131 331 4857 for details

Inchmahome Priory Open summer only

Iona Abbey Open all year, depending on ferries

Kirkwall, Bishop's Palace Open summer only

Lochleven Castle Open summer only

Meigle Museum Open April–September

St Andrews Castle Open all year. Joint entry ticket with Cathedral available

Skara Brae Summer (Joint ticket with nearby Skaill House) Winter (Skara Brae only)

Smailholm Tower Open summer only

Stanley Mills Not yet open to the public: can be viewed from the outside

Stirling Castle Summer hours – all week 9.30am to 6.00pm (last ticket sold 45 minutes before closing) Winter hours – all week 9.30am to 5.00pm (last ticket sold 45 minutes before closing)

Sweetheart Abbey Closed Thursday afternoons and Fridays in winter

Tolquhon Castle Open all summer and at weekends in winter

Trinity House Tours by arrangement; 0131 554 3289

Whithorn Priory Open Easter to October 10.30am to 5.00pm. Joint ticket by Whithorn Trust

ORKNEY

Egilsay

Skara Brae
Gurness
Kirkwall

SHETLAND

Fort Charlotte

WESTERN
ISLES

Arnol

Dun Carloway

Rodel

Dun Beag

Sueno's Stone   Elgin   Duff House

Huntly

INVERNESS

Torquhon

ABERDEEN

Lumphanan

Ruthven

Dunstaffnage   Grandtully   Meigle

Claypotts

Iona

Stanley Mills
Huntingtower   Lochleven   St Andrews

Inchmahome   Castle Campbell

Dunblane   Stirling

Cambuskenneth

Dunfermline   Aberdour   Dirleton

Kinneil   Inchcolm

Antonine Wall   Blackness   Trinity House

Linlithgow   Haddington

Castle Hill   EDINBURGH

Craigmillar   Crichton

Melrose   Smailholm

Dundonald   Kelso

Dryburgh

Cardoness   Sweetheart

Dundrennan

Whithorn

INDEX OF PLACES

 HISTORIC SCOTLAND

INDEX OF PEOPLE